"The voice in these remarkable poems belongs to a girl, a spy, a recorder of daydreams and memories of a home and a war-torn, beloved uncle, whose grisly suicide was a family secret. These poems are handprints left in cement. As Uncle Dunkel says, 'Someday strangers will know we are still partly here.' But more than 'partly here,' the poems are real presences, anchored in the holy mysteries, heartbreak, and love. Once you pick up this book, you will be unable to put it down."

–JILL PELÁEZ BAUMGAERTNER
Poetry editor, *The Christian Century*

"In the memorable voices of her younger and older selves—Kid Larkin and Eldergirl—Laurie Klein beautifully reckons with the ghosts of her family past. In these poems you will meet not only her quietly providing parents but also the war-damaged Uncle Dunkel. And snails, and a house, and a lake, and a dog, and the aptly named vesper bats. 'There are tears in things,' Virgil said. But Shakespeare said, 'Give sorrow words,' and that is what Laurie Klein has done with elegiac excellence. Until, in her words, 'all that was liquid, in the beginning, / resurfaces somewhere: / the rivers of Eden, the tears of Christ.'"

–PAUL J. WILLIS
Author of *Somewhere to Follow*

"An often haunting but ultimately hopeful story-in-verse, Laurie Klein's powerful *House of 49 Doors* explores the sacrifices we willingly or unwillingly make for others. This is a book that needs to be read, especially by those who have been trained to keep secret what pains them most. Alternating between the narrator's childhood and adult self, Klein opens hidden doors and raises locked windows. What she rediscovers are memories difficult for an adult and too heavy for a child: repercussions of war, a beloved uncle's PTSD and spiraling mental illness, a household buckling under stress. But Klein also finds in this home—amidst family and creatures with parable-like tales—a foundation of faith, joy, and love. On the threshold of grace and mercy, the author awaits. Come. Her hand is steady. Take hold."

–MARJORIE MADDOX
Author of *In the Museum of My Daughter's Mind*

House of 49 Doors

The Poiema Poetry Series

Poems are windows into worlds; windows into beauty, goodness, and truth; windows into understandings that won't twist themselves into tidy dogmatic statements; windows into experiences. We can do more than merely peer into such windows; with a little effort we can fling open the casements, and leap over the sills into the heart of these worlds. We are also led into familiar places of hurt, confusion, and disappointment, but we arrive in the poet's company. Poetry is a partnership between poet and reader, seeking together to gain something of value—to get at something important.

Ephesians 2:10 says, "We are God's workmanship . . ." *poiema* in Greek— the thing that has been made, the masterpiece, the poem. The Poiema Poetry Series presents the work of gifted poets who take Christian faith seriously, and demonstrate in whose image we have been made through their creativity and craftsmanship.

These poets are recent participants in the ancient tradition of David, Asaph, Isaiah, and John the Revelator. The thread can be followed through the centuries—through the diverse poetic visions of Dante, Bernard of Clairvaux, Donne, Herbert, Milton, Hopkins, Eliot, R. S. Thomas, and Denise Levertov—down to the poet whose work is in your hand. With the selection of this volume you are entering this enduring tradition, and as a reader contributing to it.

—D.S. Martin
Series Editor

House of 49 Doors

Entries in a Life

LAURIE KLEIN

CASCADE *Books* · Eugene, Oregon

HOUSE OF 49 DOORS
Entries in a Life

The Poiema Poetry Series

Cascade Books
An Imprint of Wipf and Stock Publishers
199 W. 8th Ave., Suite 3
Eugene, OR 97401

www.wipfandstock.com

PAPERBACK ISBN: 979-8-3852-0806-7
HARDCOVER ISBN: 979-8-3852-0807-4
EBOOK ISBN: 979-8-3852-0808-1

Cataloguing-in-Publication data:

Names: Klein, Laurie.

Title: House of 49 Doors : entries in a life / Laurie Klein

Description: Eugene, OR: Cascade Books, 2024 | The Poiema Poetry Series.

Identifiers: ISBN 979-8-3852-0806-7 (paperback) | ISBN 979-8-3852-0807-4 (hardcover) |
ISBN 979-8-3852-0808-1 (ebook)

Subjects: LCSH: subject | subject | subject | subject

Classification: CALL NUMBER 2024 (paperback) | CALL NUMBER (ebook)

VERSION NUMBER 021624

Cover photo: Lester Smith Studio, circa 1950s, used by permission of Cheryl Ache-
son.

Hold fast, I want to tell you, and myself.

For all who endure
and rise, rebuild

or . . . succumb,
in places of shelter
as well as passage,

and for those who love them

So walk.

There is only salty water behind you;
love may not come from what you love;
you cannot always choose
the door that opens your life.

–RICK MAXSON, "DO NOT DESPAIR,"
UNDER THE PEARL MOON: POEMS

Contents

Blueprint

I am a child of the heartland. I'm also the aging niece and granddaughter of builders. Raised on fairy tales, fables, and faith, my history's part magic, part riddle, part roofless awe.

Fowler House, in my day, had 49 doors and 72 windows. Now a century old, it was built on the edge of a lake dredged from swamp—waters of dubious origins that still run, metaphorically, through my veins. It's that personal. You may sense a watery presence invisibly lapping within the poems, along with the imagined voices of mercurial creatures.

You'll need to know some poems summon my preteen self. I call her Larkin. It's Irish for "fierce." Larkin's name also denotes an old-world songbird and, more tellingly, as described in the Urban dictionary, "a mystical, bird-like creature . . . stubborn and mischievous. Gentle and calm if it likes you."

Her name crops up in the titles, but I hope you'll soon recognize her voice, born of daydream and ego, hurt and hope. A voice long-silenced.

"Naming is a way of hoping," Eugene Peterson said.

One last note: My uncle and grandpa sheet-rocked over the kitchen side of one double-hung window. You'd never have known it was there, but for the casement and glass visible from our back stairs, which seems fitting for a midcentury family tragically given to secrets.

Think of me as Eldergirl, swinging open the turquoise door.

Will you join me?

Laurie Klein
December, 2023

Fowler House

I
am
standing,
still, the way
houses do, over time,
forbidden by human logic
to address *you*, dear guest, or
to try to explain how eaves fend off
more than hail, while these walls harbor
hauntings—denied by those prone to locking
mostly-forgotten bones inside family closets.
The shyest creatures around the place proffer
nimble wisdom—be it Larkin, the secret spy,
shrugging off pesky details like punctuation,
or the crazy uncle, or Fowler Lake's onetime
garfish, with teeth like tack strips for carpet.
Watch for the muskrat, turtle, the vesper bat
stitching the edges of twilight; Eldergirl too,
peering through time as if any echo, stirred,
must ricochet, ripple on and on within, then
beyond, remembrance half-founded on sand.

The Premises

*That same day Jesus went out of the house
and sat by the lake.*

–Matt 13:1 NIV

Everything Begins in Water

Take one catawampus pier, going gray,
　and several small boats thudding
　　against the bumper tires: now imagine

the *slosh*, the sinewy groan of hemp
　fed through and around
　　the boat cleats. Wind uncovers

a pang of silt. Even blind, I could
　clamber aboard. It's that real. They say
　　mooring lines should float . . .

Did they? I don't recall.
　But fore and aft, it falls to me now
　　to cast off. Recoil the ropes. And,

God as my anchor and bench mate,
　facing the dam to the west I pledge
　　all freight will be fairly borne. Only,

look past this leaky hull
　and the ghosting corrosion that clouds
　　the finish. Beyond this shore,

out where the light cascades
　sheer and true,
　　good Uncle Dunkel taught me

to row. What more can be asked
　of the long ago—save this:
　　how to remain buoyant?

Meet Kid Larkin, in Her Second Favorite Tree by the Lake, Gathering Edible Rubies

It's no use licking your fingers
There's *not* enough time
Dive-bomber robins are robbers
and they go crazy for cherries
A kid like me with a pail
gets a little flittery dodging
beaks like rockets   *Mayday   Mayday*

Maybe those birds can imagine
the jumpy ex-soldier uncle I love
who never grows out his hair
to hide that scar like a sickle moon
stuck to his temple

Me and the birds pretend
Uncle Dunkel salutes
Then he rolls out from scratch
the best ever lardy crust for pie

In my daydream he hands out
silvery whatsits with triggers
to push the pit from each gem
We heap our riches
inside his nest of dough
and we flute the edges with forks
or tiny claws

We don't have a war
What we have is a timer
that ticks like a battered engine
Sometimes the way you whistle
sugars everything   *absolutely*
hiding a woeful face

Seen from a Distance: Holiday Picnic, with Rogue Wind

What comes back from a war?

Fillips of air, swampish. Hot. Downwind
from the river, Larkin calls, "Swing with me,
Uncle Dunkel. Please?"

Love animates his long, flinty limbs
and he swings himself young again, until
two kids aim for heaven: dead even.

"Drag your feet," the pale mother cries.
The steel poles skip in their sockets:
thunk, ka-junk—blam! No, this is not

Korea. He fights his way back to the present.
Does the child see? Later, over ears of corn
seared in the husk, it seems

he has misplaced his summertime name.
The butter pools. He stares. Seeing what?
Someone, before it all congeals, say grace.

Larkin Re-daydreams the Episode
When She Went Undercover, at Church

S-h-h-h   Tuck in your shirt and lay down
We need to move cottony slow
under the pews like my mother's mop
with only the tiniest *swish-h-h*
till you feel linoleum-cold
all down the bumps of your back
Now let's paddle our hands from one seat
to the next

      like we're climbing rungs
      through shadows
      and bands of light
      on a frozen lake

This nave is my Saturday cave
where Sunday grannies will switch on
those hearing aids screwed to the pews
So don't knock a receiver off the hook
And *no talking* or Mom might scold us
for disrespect   even send us home

      Keep swimming till backglide
      turns into float with every stroke
      toward the altar she's facing now
      where she has to arrange the Gladioli

From down here each stem
is a ladder of butterflies
or a stack of gumballs with wings
about to blow bubbles
and make God laugh out loud   in church
Prayer is tiptoeing back down the aisle
our backsides spangled with angel dust

Orison, in One's Seventh Decade

It's hard to pray amid stone-clatter.
　　Lake pummels shore: slap
　　　　and shove. Every surge
　　sends a ridge collapsing while
incomers hammer, louder—
　　a mythic storm-poet's
　　　　beveled lines—enjambed,
　　without end. Squinting past
whitecaps, everything blurs,
　　save the fight water carries.
　　　　Surfaces alter. Subtext heaves.
　　Prayer ekes out small, all by itself.
Maybe boulders dislodge. Maybe,
　　silver behind your eyes becomes
　　　　splash-h-h. Something's rising . . .
　　and you're afraid. Oh, it can waver,
this faith, costly as spun glass.

What the Snapping Turtle Said

Touch with care what you don't understand:
Understand that ugly is relative, and
Relatives defend their terrain—
Terrain being code, for love-is-a-landscape.
Landscape gives and gives, then receives you,
        children of Eve—
Eve also being each day's exhale: Come,
        float into the great silence . . .

Backed into the Shallows: Father and Daughter

Memorial Day, 1961

Stand back Larkin's father warns, poised
to shift the ratchet
securing the boat winch. *No, you can't
help. That crank could break
your arm. Or my blasted hip.*
       Falling back,
she watches the prow tilt, high
on the trailer. Her father, in boat shoes,
straddles the frame, pays out line,
then jerks, gripping his wrist—
a bee? Then that menacing clunk . . .
       Oh no
ratchetsnap . . . runaway rope . . .
bonebreaker handlespin
searing the air with a huff of steam . . .
then a muffled thump: *splosh,*
the keel slips free, and
       the girl stops praying.
Pacing, her father vise-grips the sting.
Nothing broken, this time. Nothing left
to fear, the two more alike than they know,
itching to rev the engine, then,
laughing, joyride the holiday chop.

Larkin, on Building the Scream Porch

Some baby brothers can't say screen

Agent Larkin here   eavesdropping again
Dad and Mom are too loud behind their door
She says her baby brother is *fine* and he needs the work
I'm glad when Daddy gives in

For weeks Uncle Dunkel parks
one Lucky Strike behind each ear
When he visits my lemonade stand
his tools make music around his hips
and whispery tunes sneak through his teeth
He's a genie offering extra wishes
Sim sala bim   That's magic he says
for one thousand thanks

      Nail-gunnery's noisy work and I worry
      the muskrat under the willow might bolt
      leaving behind his wife and kits

Good thing tree bones hold up our new porch
hammered together with screens
to sieve out the skeeters
For sure Dad will apron up now
and every night we'll have a picnic

      Mom says so
      like a promise

In the cement my handprints are quiet
next to my uncle's   *Sh-h-h*   Imagine
he winks and whispers *Someday*
strangers will know we are still partly here

11

Dam

Two can share a rowboat:
  the girl, age eleven, while the veteran
    could be 100—her uncle,
      sole survivor of those he led.

"Something's not right," the neighbors say.
  "Do you think he hears voices?"
    Larkin believes a person can hold back
      some things, by naming others. He

holds up an oar: "Sleeve, collar,
  blade," he says, pointing them out.
    Into the rowlock it goes. "See?
      No slippage."

Then, with a grin: "Helps the guy
  manning the paddles
    to keep his grip." All she knows?
      A boat the color of dirty nickels

flies like a warrior's arrow
  unzipping the atmosphere:
    each stroke opens
      a swirling hole. How deep,

below the keel, does emptiness go?
  "I've got you," he says,
    as if he hears the voice
      inside *her* head. Two can pause

under a weeping willow
  that moves like a grass skirt,
    with roots, at the edge
      of the spillway. Do you know

where happiness starts?
  With one hushed glide
    beneath green petticoats, where
      fractured light sieves over skin

and reflections swarm over leaves
  like fireflies. You can give a person
    a new name—which today
      might be Merlin—unless

wind slues your vessel
  into the current, drawing you pell-mell
    toward that awful blue roar like a gale
      where everything crashes

and falls while he rows and rows
  to escape the thundering
    dam, knuckles slick with spray,
      his gaze, wild. *This* is slippage.

Almost a Way to Say Sorry

Yes, we survived the near-runaway
boat—but oh, how my uncle trembled,
rowing us home. Spooked,

afterward, I waded into the shallows,
shanghaied a leech, dropped it
into a paper cup. Maybe I salted

that pulsing brocade because
children who try to protect
their grownups from flashbacks

sometimes elect a scapegoat.
I'd like to apologize now
for those innocent garments of flesh

that fizzed and split,
little vestments of foam
forever minus their tassels.

What the Muskrat Said

Mend the lodge. Mentor the kits.
Understand teeth are the final gateway.
Stalk the whispering flutes of air
        hidden within common reeds.
Kiss an overlooked wonder: webbing.
Relish the numberless psalm
        formerly known as *swim.*
Amen the snails!
Tail every floating tendril of glory . . .

Ha brakha dabra: "The blessing has spoken."

Shotgun Hall

He is near, right at the door.

–Matt 24:33b BSB

Larkin's Hijinks Aquarium
(complete with mirrored hall tree and closet)

Ignore our raggedy hedge and skip
right between Mister Blue Spruce
and his dying missus
Climb the steps to the porch
and drag each shoe
over the boot scraper
shaped like a dachshund

       The blade's supposed to be hackles I guess
       My wiener dog Hildegaard isn't fooled
       That's where she piddles

Here's the brass knob   *Ta-da*
Four walls make a kid-size aquarium
with windows or mirrors on every side
If you have a bottle of pop
cork it tight with your thumb
and joggle it high as a wand
Abra-ka-doozel   Geysers

       Lemon-lime rain
       Razzle and dazzle
       Star-spangliest room in the house

Twirl with me inside a diamond

Eldergirl: A Family with Four Back Doors Has Something to Hide

Face east with me, your back to the lake. Can you
smell those tawny bricks, a century old—dust
and clay and pulverized shale

mortared with sorrow? Fountaining high,
forsythia half-shrouds the way in,
like a thousand hatchlings, each goldfinch

a-flutter among the limbs. I'd invite you in, but
my gentle mother would have to apologize.
This is a rich man's house, from the front.

Ballooning backyard screens escape their brads.
Between doors one and two,
the first window you'd see, boarded over

on one side, would barely reflect
your image—your passage
blurred, like an eye with a cataract.

Street Level

Jesus entered a house and did not want anyone to know it;
yet he could not keep his presence a secret.

–Mark 7:24b NIV

Hindsight

God haunted our stairwell at night
with a shadowy stance
hard to perceive. Not once

did I see my parents linger within
that shotgun hall. It was,
for me, a wishing womb, glassed in

by seven French doors,
where the pendant light swung
and stuttered with water whenever

someone showered too long—
the bulb, a faerie ship in a bottled squall,
fritzing on—off. How early we learn

to step back, rather than forth,
convinced *What we are,*
already, cannot be undone.

In the catch of memory's breath,
reclamation goes on:
a nail drops out of the paneling.

About Barbs, Then and Now

> KID LARKIN
> (twirling a pigtail)

Zip on your jacket *fast*
with a whoop and holler
So what if you're small
Be an angel a spy a jumping bean
Quick-shinny that one-pie tree
and bucket up cherries   mmMMM
And if loudmouth jays rain down
bluer than bullets
just say the Our Father
no matter what happens
and Go kid   Reap it

> ELDERGIRL
> (twirling a cane)

I grew up believing in ovens
and pie's tangy sweetness, pulsing
through slits. I still make a wish
on the point of each slice—even after
my father broke his tooth on a cherry stone.
"Hurray! Finding a pit means a kiss for the cook,"
my mother enthused, misreading
the damage. His dead-eyed comeback
bit deep. Payback
is an arrowhead zinging through glare,
a missile, heat-seeking a throat.

Archer, Which Animal Has the Most Teeth?

Larkin and Uncle Dunkel, in the living room

No, *not* the crocodile, Larkin says. Her uncle plucks
his bowstring, with every guess—(trying, *twang,*
taking pains, to play along): "Catfish. Dolphin? . . . Shark!"

        Nope. Her creature can block out the whole world,
        sleep for three years—(*his* hourly wish,
        after the war). He sees his string needs waxing

        lest he misfire. She winks, adding
        her shell-dweller moves on its own juice, one mile
        in thirty-three hours—(*like finally taking the ridge* he thinks,

        armored bodies coiled around guns
        in the retching dark: the mud, the labored,
        uphill crawl). He remembers the orphans of war

                and then, Aesop's hungering child—
                who once ignited a blaze, to roast
                snails in a pan. They *squeeed* and hissed.

                What possessed them he wonders,
                to muster the heart to whistle
                when their houses were burning?

        Twang. His guess is a question: "How many teeth
        per SNAIL?" She grins. Up to 20,000 per tongue,
        she announces. His jaw drops. O how she loves

to amaze him. Promise we'll do this
forever, she says. The man sets his weapon
aside—(taking pains, to smile).

What the Snail Said . . . (eventually)

Blessed are those who love the earth
with their feet as they walk.

–Erin Geesaman-Rabke

Sundown calls a goo-mover forth. I could be
Nature's un-ribboning scripture
      (all spit 'n shine) or
A seeker's itchy foot, re-pilgriming time. Only
Ingenious eyes retract. Watch. Wherever
Longing paves the way, the most passionate
S t r e t c h often entails the lifelong seep . . .

While Swimming Laps, Eldergirl Remembers Her Childhood Tree House

Once upon a tree, time shed
its yellowing gloves,

and in my freckled, believing
hands, those oblong leaves

became funnels for fireflies,
each tenderly rolled cone

painstakingly stitched
closed, with a twig. I remember,

now, during lightless times,
those teeming jewels no longer

afloat in autumn twilight. And,
like an exile, I keep feeling around for

the old contours. Shelter. Mostly,
the twinkling.

The Secret Bellyfoot Opera,
under the Dining Room Window

A rout, a walk, an *escargatoire*
  of snails—do you envy their elasticity?
    To each, an aria, tender antennae perceiving,
      smelling and feeling, heeding
      an orchestration, inborn: Seek. Glean.
    But this thirst! Dare we risk
  spiraling outward, onward, a frangible
ode-in-motion? Dear Earth, why show us
  these rippling, quicksilver guides,
    their boneless glide,
      each fearless right-angle ascent
      with a cellular faith's acrobatic
    sheen—even upside-down? Surely,
  an ancient desert mother advised,
Your shell *will teach you everything.*

Larkin's Mom, in Her Kitchen, at Twilight

With thanks to J.B. Priestly

She sits as one might in a pew, watching
  the nest, with its on-and-off robin
    stockinged in brown, the bright apron
      a blur. So many errands.

    When the bird finally settles,
    How taxing the woman thinks,
  to brood alone over the future, beating
hearts pressed into the gap.

Yet don't the living always
mother something or other,
enact the urgent to-do alongside
the no-can-do? Tail feathers flick,
tick, rhythmic as household
clockwork—apt to run down.
Ever-wed to the winding key,
inside its carved house of wood

the cuckoo is bound to return.
  And the snail-eating robin will come
    to know the spectator's face. Delicate
      trust unfurls despite querulous sparrows

    or staggering bills for a money-pit house.
   Nod, if you'd like to be found faithful,
  unfazed by a hectoring world. Just once,
to glow, as if candled: *innocent as an egg.*

One Whole Room for a Lonesome Piano

The sunroom calls *Yoo-hoo* on rainy nights
when sixteen windows and four French doors
change into mirrors   They help me practice
my not so grand jetés   And pliés

> Teacher said *The true ballerina speaks*
> *by creating a hush   Come back*
> *when you can pay attention*

Some teachers forget ideas leap

Imagine an old old woman appears
waving a wand   *Poof*   Her dark cape swirls
and never once does she say
Try moving like water that shivers with light
But that's what she means

Watch her vanish behind the piano
That's when my foot pushes a pedal down
and chords shimmer into steps
as my hands dance over the keys
till the wishing cloud scoots my way
and one baby star blinks along in time

But Dad interrupts   And I see
what my teacher meant   Feet go numb
Fingers can't find the music
Never mind Water Dancer   Everyone knows
radiators make good kneelers
Slow-twirl the dogleg crank
till every weeping window becomes
a once-upon-a-time bridge   Now
let in the mist

Radiator, Seen from a Distance

And here is the weekend
father of Fowler House,
stooping to bleed
the cast iron rads,
room by room—
the kitchen, first:
       snug key into valve,
       expel pent-up steam.
The smallest airlock
can block warmth: no rising,
no moving outward.
But monitor that ensuing *his-s-s* . . .
Sleeve pulled tight
over your wrist,
hold steady an empty cup
to catch the welling,
there, at the valve's throat,
and smile, lest duty alone
swamp
what was meant as love.

Eldergirl Tries to Imagine Verna, Uncle Dunkel's Fiancée, in Her Kitchen

After the cloudburst, rainworms
cluster on pavements, almost
legible, their italics a damp rehearsal
for language. Verna thinks
those scrawls resemble *his*: "The soldier's

soul," he wrote, from Korea,
"seems doomed to writhe,
despairing of heaven—
the God we believe in
being the one we'll meet."

Beyond her kitchen,
twilight narrows its louvers. If only
his mind could rest. But
he wants to spare her—maybe that's all
he has left. So, is this a kindness?

Ringless, Verna crumples his letter,
turns from the burrowing cursive
of grief, incited by horror. She's tired.
No more wringing her hands, lamenting
their feet of clay, the careless rain.

Evening Walk, Sleet Pending (dachshund version)

How to ditch this ridiculous sweater?
If I rumble that bush in hopes of a snag . . .
Low bellies chill; better stay dressed.
Das ist mein Leben, "This is my life": bodily
Ensuring my girl is warm every night. *I*
Guard her. *Ach,* we should be home!
All this wooly to-do over thin fur, short legs.
And hypothermia. Brrr. Please, freezing
Rain, hound us back home before Meister
Dad ventures too far. She might be shivering.

Kid Larkin, Being Interviewed on Pretend TV, Explains "Where We Eat"

Where we eat is a perfect lookout
for me and my dog
It's wrapped in long windows
and bare brick walls

        meaning no insulation
        my best uncle says

Wind makes rattlepane glass
shiver inside the frames
but he'll fix things up for us
when it's not so stormy
making a nook like a snow globe
attached to our castle with 49 doors

Meanwhile I'm coming loose
in my chair because
whether snow falls in the yard
or sneaks through the cracks
saying grace with Dad
also means trading puns

That's when the side-by-side
twinkling appears   *Alakazam*
Like two fireflies switching on and off
behind his big black glasses

Eldergirl, between Tables

I miss that massive, carved antique,
those storied tastes of home arrayed
across added leaves, the holiday squabbles,
lefse. Ancestral meatballs.

Was the first table of all volcanic—
hell-hot magma, hardened to stone,
and set for three in the garden,
later forbidden? Never forgotten.

What is it with mealtimes
and families, at war? King David's
al fresco lunch, per God's
invitation, meant feasting his foes.

And Mary, the chosen host
for the holiest DNA of all time
presided in peace though
beset by tiny elbows and heels. Did she

foresee one Gentile mother's plea
in the name of crumbs
for the hungry, who argued
for every outsider's worth

to be reclaimed? Love, pull out
another chair, easing what seethes
among and within us. Bid us
reenter the dear, collective Amen.

Larkin Hates that a Wintertime Dad Can Forget to Come Home for Supper

Everything's twice as bad tonight
when the bat zooms in
thwapping the windows and walls
Poor Mom yanks open the clothes chute
then runs for the broom

> *Whoos-h-h*   So much for the bat
> doomed to wait for Dad in the basement

When Dad has too many meetings   we clean
our new turquoise stove and matching fridge
Since this is my mother's favorite color
most days I wear azure or teal aqua jade
and those big chrome knobs that landed one night
like flying saucers on all her new cupboards
are funhouse mirrors where I see myself blue

> Too bad every door and drawer
> gets gnawed by Hildegaard's teeth
> She likes changing the edges of things
> Dad says she'd better live up to
> her High German name
> for a lowdown dog

Bedtime soon   and he's *still* not here
That's a lucky break for the bat
But one of these days my dog
and I might stop waiting around

What the Vesper Bat Said

The family vespertilionidae
wishes to thank Larkin's father
for setting its poet free

Venerating the upside-down—it's like faith:
Ever-endangered. Claws? These are currycombs,
Serving the sleek. Are we quill-fingered,
Pennyweight hucksters of doom? Lean closer.
Even on moonless nights, we revel,
Regrouping by day, wing to pleated wing.
Tonight, tasting pure, high-wire tingle, yes,
I tense, chilled, until some great felicity
Lifts me, from flit through dip to starry soar
Inscribing the skies . . . What? Oh, the holy
Omnipotence makes us kin: we too have
Navels. We stay up. We listen in.
Intent upon pollination, may we
Dare the boundless—abounding
Awe, seeding the darkness,
Euphoric . . . as diving blind.

Dive: After Supper, Larkin Relives the Kiwanis Swim Meet

Your legs should jackknife my uncle says
then extend with a snap
Like his folding ruler   but human   Watch me
touch my toes   In my new navy blue suit
I feel speedy and sleek as his Streamliner coupe

Starting whistles turn feet into springs
and every girl's elbows hinge and reach
till the water's a storm and my teammate cheers
but I am the last one back to the pier
She power-dives over my head
with a perfect *snap*   Beats me why I entered
this stupid relay   Water up my nose
I practice the dead man's float so I don't have to watch
the winners wave their blue ribbon

But a draggle of lakeweed climbs my neck
like a dying thing I'm afraid to touch
And words never meant to be overheard
replay in my head

> *Uncle D telling Dad about*
> *   night patrols with his bayonet*
> *hating that oily brown river in Asia*
> *   swollen with corpses*

I am not quick in the water   But I believe
my uncle was made for grasping the measure of things
like a kid's hope on her big day

We're all drowning a little he says afterward
and he lays two snail shells in my wrinkly palms
You and me don't need prizes

Clothes Chute

And it came to pass . . .

Vesper Bat, Then and Now

KID LARKIN, 1963

A blur of fur
trapezes
through Mom's new kitchen
She ducks and I drop
her favorite gravy boat
Smithereens everywhere
One china bridge between willows
and true-blue birds
are all that is left

And the crying

Cradling the damage
I stay down on one knee
calling *Hey Flitterwhiz*
Watch out for the broom
Mom's at bat
and she can be fierce   Zip
zag   you flit from our fridge
to the sill over the sink
where her snow globes
and paperweights dream

yet nothing is broken
I've tried gluing things
back together   At our house
seems like somebody's broom
forever bruises the air

ELDERGIRL, 2023

Vesper bat, you must have

half-collapsed that night,
wing bones cocked for a dive
as you slipped through a door.
Did your swivel ears
tune out irrelevant sounds,
the way a preteen ignores
unwanted signals? Sometimes,
my grownups answered echoes
they only imagined.
Maybe my mother, flailing
her broom, never saw
I was trapped: ever the runt
in class, seldom in sync. Tell me,

breakneck aerobat,
did you weave and rise
for both of us, take on
that picture window reflecting
a room with no escape?

Dusk to dawn, you and your kind
pollinate our planet,
like mothers, who tend the small.
Thank you for mangos, avocados,
cacaos. Pollination swoops,
and you remind me: mostly,
our parents mean well.

Stairwell

Is not my house right with God?

−2 Sam 23:5a BSB

Larkin, En Route to the Second Floor, Inventories Her Elbows

Climb into my indoor treehouse
here on the mirrored landing where
if I could be Tinkerbell   for a single day
you would call me the perfect Mender of Things

There's a stain glass stork with an awkward gap
where the melty lead is pulling away
and a soup tureen missing its lid holds
plastic flowers that droop with dust

> Don't mind the smeary pupcus
> down low on the mirror
> Hildy keeps me company in between floors
> as if we are the last two fairies on earth

But tonight when I twirl   my elbows look weird
like the meat man downtown
crammed a skipping rock inside the stretchy skins
of two sausages   Knobs

I have *knobs* inside my sleeves

And each magic word I know fizzles
till I am sick to my lonely bones
How did this happen to me
the kid of a mother with movie star arms

Magic, beyond the Landing: Or, What the Fireflies Said

Fliz-z-z—watch this! We live to unravel light—
Introducing . . . us! Spellbinders. Gold leaf
Romeos, lofting candles. Do you know
Ephemeralese? Read our poets,
Fluent in glimmer. Sure, the arc stutters;
Lives flicker. But sequin confetti
Itches to glitz most *everything*! Huzzah,
Erratic dazzle! Winking cinders, arise:
Spangle lawns. Sky. The lone soul night.

Eldergirl Remembers the Magi

For the wordless patience
of plastic wise men—
airbrushed in turquoise,
cobalt, and violet-gold,
meant to proceed
from our landing, step
by step, day after day,
to the family crèche
(figures I drop-kicked,
downstairs, behind
Mom's back)—I pledge
these lines on my knees
in apology, shivering
now, as the star comes for me.

A House Like A Shawl

Of course, we must all
unravel, as we gravely
mouth the verbs of change,
until ego resists no more
than a garment,

sloughed. May our souls,
exposed, finally forgo
shoring up gaps,
as if we can somehow
repair one blessèd thing. Maybe

these closet selves, no more
substantial than April air
crocheted into a shawl,
only need to be shouldered,
held again to the breastbone.

Half-flight, to the Next Story

*Don't you know that you yourselves
are God's temple?*

−1 Cor 3:16 NIV

Larkin, in Bed with the Flu, Relives that Day at the River, without Her Dog

No one ever said
one knee-caving bellow
could root a kid to the spot
Here in this almighty murk of a river
you can't even see the bottom

Some vacation

I miss Hildy's waggery self
Big ole barge chunters past
and a girl plugs her ears
but the horn keeps going and blowing
as waves slap my thighs like they know
I fudged my swim test

Up at the cottage Uncle Dunkel helps Mom
unjacket potatoes for supper
No one sees the bully next door
duck underwater
He lobs a big sucking gob of muck
all down my front and
no one needs to say ugly

I smell like fish eggs and
things that died in the dark
all of me stained
by gooze the river made up
like a stinking lie
layer by layer laying it down
but not so deep
that meanness can't reach it

Larkin's Mom, Kneeling, in Her Bedroom

Someone has to keep watch. The dog's too old.
Dear crow on your nest, in the blue spruce,
your whole body vibrates, but vertically,
like a feathered piston. Should I
look away? I could ignore

your beak, probing for faults.
Between prying and poking,
too many mothers
upend their fragile homes.

Perhaps, little wife, you embody
acceptance: for every weakness,
exposed, your pliant
sutures go in. Is this prayer?

Larkin says *Birds have secret knees,*
under their feathers. Bowing,
I feel less alone. Sister crow,
in guarding our young,
let us also repair what we can.

That Dark and Stormy Night,
with a Hound Dog Named Brahms

Shuffle and *scre-e-e-k*   Ghost feet
inch up the attic stairs
past the awful hole that could
swallow a leg   *s-s-s-thukh*
ankle to hip   Shivery under the quilt
my legs cycle for warmth till my dog yips

Wind   plays crack-the-whip in the treetops
Wind   fires rain like nails at my window
Wind   but this time not a tornado

Ka-blam   Lightning zaps the big elm
and runs down the trunk like a squirrel on fire
Ground is supposed to swallow the power
but all that *ziz-z-z* must be gouging
a path to the neighbor's wall
because *their* attic bursts into flames

You're okay Mom says and her hug
muffles the dog next door
He's nearly howling his spots off
Hildegaard lays her chin on my feet
and we let the hound cry for us all   *Good boy*
Good ole Brahms   Yowl

Downsizing, 2023

One small cedar box. Gone. All that brass:
fairy tale hinges and hasp, two chains to counter
the lid's weight. Perhaps its creator,

my uncle, knew I'd need something to carry
close to my chest, away from the burning house
he'd become. *Crafts for crazies* he called it.

Did I make that up? There was a room
with supplies: tiles like thumbnails
gnawed to the quick, their colors

resembling smoke and bones, blood,
glints of embedded metal. Shades of war.
Brushes and bottles of glue held things together,

all those months he was forced
to forfeit his tool belt,
that wide, flat pencil over one ear,

and me. For sixty years, I kept it.
Now I am missing
that box, smelling faintly of cedar and love.

Larkin and the Hope Chest

Chintz Schmintz   Not what *I'd* pick
Mom wants it tight and smooth as a sheet
with no wrinkles at all   She says *We're making*
a window seat for daydreams and books

This could take all day and a million tacks
Busy hands are happy hands she adds
and *No eyerolls please*   I say
I'm allergic to stretching

She laughs and hands me a pie plate
putting me in charge of the metal thorns
There's upholstery foam and a roll of fluff
and a cedar box big as a kid's coffin

What does it mean to force a cushion
over the hope chest she emptied   *Thump*
Bam   She hammers and hammers   I handle
the ammunition   though I'd rather go

swimming   But Dad saw a garfish
gnashing its wicked jaws near our pier   So
we slave away till he finally comes home
to change   He stands outside

with his big harpoon   Dad waits like a hero
somebody cut from the sky with tinsnips
For now   he's still here   keeping us safe
keeping us guessing

Belated Remembrance

After Wendell Berry

Feeling half-swamped
by runaway currents, Larkin,
at seventy-three, backstrokes
through time to press her palms
once again against the delicate skin
of the gingko tree, the one
and only, in her hometown.
Rooted in siltish soil,
come autumn it shadowed
the western wall of the church,
flaunting 10,000 golden fans:
a waving descendant her uncle said,
of the oldest tree
to inhabit the earth. Daydream
replays three fluting sighs
of a mourning dove,
high in the canopy, alive again,
with rustling endearments—yet
ghostly, too, as his unseen hand
almost rocks her skiff of a self.

Eldergirl, Running a Bath

One story is good, until another is told.
–Aesop

I remember my girlish feet
burrowed in pea gravel, sun-struck
with gleam—those shifting caves
cradling my soles,
       arches, insteps.
Was it wrong to ask for a fish
if my father harbored a snake,
his hushed pursuit of wealth
       stealthy
as silt? I have carried that hidden,
downriver slither, felt it settle
its coils in my gut,
       heisting time.
But those stones, yearly delivered:
perhaps their amber shimmer
absolved him, loved him,
       a man wading onward,
barefoot, raking that pebbled carpet,
pale as kernels cut from a cob.
It doesn't die, this wanting:
the clean dive, bubbles rushing up.

The Psalm Formerly Known as *Swim*, for Two Voices (then, and now)

KID LARKIN:
(poised to dive)

Watch me turn into a knife
the second my toes leave the pier
No running start on slaprattle boards
loud as a drum roll   Today I'm a warrior niece
squinching one eye
as I double-dog-dare my shivery self
to slice through the surface
Humbubbles will rise like helium
to soothe a tongue that gets snippy
and hurts Mom's feelings
First the plunge   then silvery ripplets
smoothing and smoothing over the cut

ELDERGIRL:
(floating)

Awash with decades, these sinews forget
how svelte the body can still feel. Amphibian, almost.
Water's immersive embrace takes me in
like a mother. Skin revives! How deliciously
fluent I am, in propulsion. Each flutter kick syncs
with a sculling palm. Have I always known
how to arch and flex, streamline
the anthem of lungs to a modest surf,
inside the shell of my skull? What if
I call this . . . healing?—piercing
as birdsong my uncle might have heard
near the river of death, during a lull
in the war, remembered. Then forgotten.

Eldergirl, on the Mystery of Physics

They still patrol the Rock River, at dusk,
those vesper bats, dodging
the *hum-plunk* of fishline—perhaps, a Rebel
CrickHopper's wink, underwater. Imagine

my uncle and best-friend Louie, angling
for bluegills: boys who compared toejam,
worried their scabs; later, as teens,
springing mutts from the dogcatcher's van.

Along came Verna, a Roman candle,
all limbs and ribs. She was touchwood, smoldering
punk: pure fuel. Guys shot sparks
whenever she smiled. *Anything biting* she'd ask—

a sheath of a voice, like rolled suede. Later,
after my uncle's tour of duty, did she ever
visit the bait shop? Eye the old lures?
What of the promised house? And her man,

unhooked from reality: bats, storming his belfry,
cattails morphing to bayonets, particles
smashing together—
one version of the beginning.

Larkin's First-Ever, Top-Secret Mailbox

clank   k-s-s-s   Radiators
make the best cover for working spies
Inside our bluest room with the fake Monet
my mother's new sink matches
her giant bottle of Milk of Magnesia
Rule number one is *Dry the sink after you use it*

but don't use the washcloths rolled up like dolls
And don't touch the little seashell soaps
in the candy jar   which might burn less
than the bar of Castile she lays on your sassy tongue

Don't tell anyone the keyhole is jammed
with vitamins I only pretended to swallow
ever since I poked one and yellow goo came out
Good thing they collapse when I shove them in

One loose tile under the door lifts out
That's where I hide notes   about parents and war
and the garfish lurching around our pier
Today I wrote Aesop   in care of God
Dear animal man   Please help us
So far   no answer

What the Garfish Said

It all depends on the point of view,
and who tells the story.

–Aesop

Glory like mine packs fangs. Check out
      these choppers: pure
Ambush, customized for a living torpedo.
      Feel reverent yet? Ah,
Repelled. Maybe you think
      I'm a brooding, Jurassic
Freak. No one numbers
      these babies—canines, molars,
Incisors that multiply, row after row,
      lifelong—like shards of
Shekinah, adorning needle-nose jaws.
      Yo, grok this: hallowèd,
Hallowèd be his perilous innovation.
      Amen? Oh yeah.

Operation Spygirl

Kids like me keep watch
for signs of divorce
since a dad half cross-eyed with pain
from a fall he took at my age
can't always be patient

       Mom says his spine
       was one big twist
       That's why he limps
       That's why his freckle-bomb
       knees ache

Today when a nosy breeze
nudges open the bathroom door
I should look away
because Dad holds Mom like a baby
then slowly lowers her into the tub

       With her bandages off
       after the operation
       her legs are tornado colors
       Where varicose veins used to be
       scabs look like fireworks
       and water beads up
       like even her skin is crying

Mom flops sideways against the tile
and I can't look away as Dad kneels down
all crooked   He dips the blue rag again
and again   Humming softly
he soaps and rinses her perfect back

There must be a way to listen

like a small body of water,
reflective face, upturned: benign,
an entity of acceptance.

Water embraces the sunken. The near-dying
as well as the thriving stir, like plants
practicing grace as they lean on the current.

Let me be a haven, where shared sediments
settle. Where buoyancy reasserts itself.
Where you will beckon the weathered vessel,
and I will coax the reluctant toe.
We'll soften the chipped margins of shells,
castoffs, the chronically stony. Encompassed,

eased, the survivor rises
the way a trout breaks from silence, to surface,
old hooks and lines ingrown, jaws half-trussed—

wounds revealed, by one seeking a witness.
What was it the risen one said? Hark.
Flow and do likewise.

Boatman

*Can a man row long enough
to breach the roaring?*

Diamonds dripped from the oars
when my uncle taught me the strokes: catch,
drive, recovery. For the schizophrenic, nearing
the spillway, the dam's thunderous
clamor must have sounded like enemies
urging the plummet. Or was it white noise.
A lullaby? Lac La Belle dazzled beyond,
the island hemmed in by floating blooms.

Ah, Night Boatman of Souls, even now
receive our coin. Thanks to my uncle,
I mastered the hard turn,
the simultaneous push and pry. I learned
to whistle. *Wet your lips* he said.
*Raise your eyebrows and whisper
Q, Q—over and over: adjust the pucker
until music breaks free.*

Did he still whistle, after
the sanitorium? Silences fell
between his rationed words,
as if, hounded by inner voices,
he'd already shipped oars, somewhere
amid that carpet of lilies: a man,
alone, enduring the tenacious roar.

Larkin, in Her Socks, Hands on Ears

A short kid wants shoes that *move*
airy as cooked clouds on a lemon pie
They float me above the snark
and grazzle of grownups
who stump around in a huff

Rainwords hiss
through my pink gingham walls
Dad's good at zingers
They spritzle like lightning on stilts
Answers from Mom sigh   like a whistle
losing its way in the dark

Sometimes our house is a radio
choking on static
like WTMJ in a storm
except it's people who go on the fritz
This is just one secret I keep

This is the reason I turn
the big glass knob and step into my closet
I am looking for pillowy tongues
and soft red laces   and soles that
leave an impression I can count on

Vesper Bat

Emerging from a makeshift closet
under the eaves, the dubious parson of night

adjusts his little cassock of fur, coolly
unfurling the long, dark sleeves. He forgoes

his usual parish of air, flitting instead
across our inmost chancel of sleep, rousing

> the old ache—
> the one we told no one

about . . .
And just like that,

after all these years,
a sigh chafes like gravel,

and perhaps the dream bat, bearing
witness, echolocates the scar,

enwrapping hurt in widening,
wordless arcs. Perhaps we feel

heard, seen—by a fellow creature
briefly ordained for the care of souls.

Agent Larkin Hides a Letter
under the Loose Bathroom Tile

Dear Uncle Dunkel   *How could you*
Since you died
it's like everything's underwater
Grownups pretend-swim
Especially your mother
Even *mine* for crying out loud
your big sister

Only three days to Christmas
and Nana ties on her apron
Crackers collapse into dust
with blows from her rolling pin
Mom breaks egg after egg
They measure out spices
to make the meatballs
and I smell gingery pepper
tumbled with nutmeg   as usual

They are working the cold raw meat
in separate bowls
glinty with blood and animal fat
One batch with onions   like always

They mix everything up
No one says Jesus is coming
and you are gone   Dear uncle
their fingers under the faucet twist
and scrub at the sickly
grease I can smell from here

Eldergirl, on Forgetting

1964, the year's longest night

Scattershot: that's how my father spoke.
Half-dazed. Wind rattled the cherry tree.
Branches snapped. Even then,
I perceived pivotal moments the way
they were lit—my bedside lamp
shorting out, his face receding
in spasms, his words like migraines
I still get: neon wheels and flares.

A tree, he'd said. Then my uncle's name.
No need to check his wrists,
for a pulse: Nothing,

that's what I said, quiet as film
curled in its can, on which
images would later develop,
floating face-up.

To this day I distrust the winter solstice,
missing those two men I adored, who hoarded
their separate wars, likely
retold scenes only with comrades
who'd never ask how many
they'd killed. Which made them feel

safe. But trauma's fumes, stealthy
as fixatives, escape their containers.
Strangers cut down the cherry tree,
leaving the stump. And me?
Entrusted with horror, that night I absorbed
all. Unaware I'd grown up.

Darkroom

Say a grisly scene imprints,
cell-deep. Dear witness,
we absorbed it back then,
why reagitate the negative now,
risking more details?

Think back: old accusations,
that swung fist. Soundtrack of tears,
or taunting—whatever your story,
the real cause still underexposed.

Sometimes we prefer fog
and shadows. I insist
on hanging my worst memory
upside down, behind
the mind's darkest cupboard,

lest heartbreak
dare the second look . . .
Truth? Or edgeless
translucence, then nothing.

Seen from a Distance: Father, Daughter, Uncle

He does not tell her
if it was an elm, an oak,
or sycamore; or if
the birds stopped singing.
He does not tell her
if the cop found a note;
or what will become
of the barbed wire—although
he describes that phone call,
at dawn, five days before
Christmas, miles of black ice,
the Pontiac fishtailing all the way
to the next county. He confides
he helped release the body,
into the spattered snow.

All her life, he has told her *Secrets
breed lies.* Now he says
*Mom and Nana must never know
how it was done. Do you understand?
It would kill them.* And the child,
at her father's behest, agrees
to conceal this rot-blossom shame,
within their family tree. *Call it loyalty*
he says. *A final kindness.*

No more.

Say instead, how insidious, how lonely
and taxing, that long compliance,
holding back the unthinkable,
each small evasion, erosive. The girl
is haunted by trees. Ring by ring,
a sycamore's aging trunk deletes
its own childhood—self-hollowing—while

69

the bark keeps peeling back,
back to the hues of youth. Poor heart,
rest now. Hear the mourning dove cry *Uncle*.

Eldergirl Imagines a Mourning Dove's Invitation

Meet me by the pine, weeping seeds for us.
O forsaken one, can fallen cones assuage our pain?
Under every thorny lip,
Resurrection slumbers; we could split a woody tongue,
Naming who is gone. Once upon a grave,
I watched a body dwindle, as if
Nesting, into earth. Goodbye, my best companion. No more
Grayed pearl, mauve-rose. Teal eye rim. Crimson toes.
                    Selah   *Selah-h-h*
Dare we peck among the broken, left unsung?
O forlorning, laid aside, must mourning now be
Veiled? Come bow beneath the rain with me, where
Every parting bears a cost and every seed, its wing.

Larkin, Gripping the Red Leash, at the Clinic

No matter how gently they say *You're old enough now*
to understand   this kind of sad feels longer
than all the dogs in the world lining up

Hildegaard is pure dachshund 100 percent
She has forever eyes like my uncle
and toenails blacker than locust thorns
You have to make sure she never
jumps off the couch too fast for that bacon
you crammed in your pocket at breakfast

Dogs love bacon   But she got caught
in the fringe and I thought
I untangled her foot in time
But her extralong back got hurt
and she couldn't get up

I should have eaten that bacon
It's my fault she can't walk
Now she's shaking so hard
her love is all bumps and bones under my hand
and her droozy eyes make my breathing hurt

We'll let her sleep now Dad says

I am holding onto the leash instead of his hand
and I keep walking backwards until
the door shuts   and the clouds open up
and all around there is drowning
Forever is just so long

Attic

So Jesus went to her,
and took her hand,
and helped her up.

Mark 1:31 NIV

Eldergirl, Climbing

Webs, flies, husks of bees. I remember
the dormer window, shaped like a house,
flung open. No screens. No doors.
No safety bar: a three-story drop. I remember
studs. Spaces between. My skeleton
playhouse beckoned, its cavern suggesting
the ribs of a whale. A rubbery ghost
kept watch—that World War II diving suit,
slung from a rafter. No ponderous
helmet studded with glass portals,
and no snaking hose,
with its hissing feed of air. I remember
the collar's metallic leer, like
a jack-o'-lantern. Oh yes, an effigy
shadowed those floorboards,
sole-deep in dust. Back then,
no one explained "submersible." Or
the bulky belt, cracked in places,
those pockets for ballast, gaping. Where
did those heavy weights go? I think
of my father and uncle,
honors and medals, squirreled away,
discovered decades after they died,
and now, no one left to unriddle
heroic deeds or regrets or
that awful relic, suspended.

Larkin, in the Attic Lookout

She's dying for real
Bet Mister Blue Spruce
will miss his withery missus
I thought they'd forever
bookend our house

Wind over the dam
blows hard as a slap
and together they tame
the cold and commotion
Together they make a lullaby

Strangers will chop down
comfort the color of rust and sky
Bet they'll have tin ears
Bet they won't hear
her final hum

Words I keep falling through hiss
You promised to never tell Mom
I worry Dad might have used
my uncle's tinsnips
to cut him down from the tree

Now the workmen rev their saws
Our mother-tree sways
Goodbye rock-a-bye song
holding us all
with broken arms

Profile

Why, moon halo
in heaven, must you suggest
Nana's cameo—milky features
pinned against black silk? She
seems near tonight, her nimbus
of hair loosed from the usual
French twist, pale and flyaway-fine,
prone to snarl. I think of

her lost son, bent on ending
his life—already hell—thus,
hell-bound, or so said
the people at church.

So, then what? Guilt must be
boar-bristled, every night,
then tightly braided. Come mornings,
till Nana was almost 105,

perhaps she ran that cameo's barb
through the silvering strands
still hugging her skull. Perhaps
she collected traces of oil

to ease the daily pierce—brooch
to blouse. See her set
the clasp, with its tiny wheel,
half-spun, near her heart,
her boy's face, a second moon
in the dark, finally serene,
akin to the Prince we call
Peace, glimpsed from the side.

Peripheral

Maybe my sorrow is for
all the lost and fallen things.
–Loretta Diane Walker

And when the dead will not cease
speaking? Let us stoop,
clear a ring of raw earth
around their graves, tamp in
a woolly herb like creeping
thyme. Half-buried,
gilt saucers ransomed
from backyard sales
form a porcelain hem. Call this
a truce. Or a conversation.
The soul's makeshift frame, for loss.

No grave? Cut the buckle
off the frayed red leash.
Gather sea glass alongside
orphaned buttons and
foreign coins. Sometimes
goodbyes coil inward before
spiraling outward, so come,
adhere your emblems
amid all that is shattered:
make your mosaic
a font, for the fugitive rain.

Dunkelheit

After Yusef Kumunyakaa

German noun (singular, feminine),
meaning "absence of light"

My rangy uncle hung
like an airborne wallow of fog
engulfing a valley. No. He hung
like a migrant's emptied sack.
Time passed. I pictured a rolled carpet slung
between movers. Still, no face. Once,
he hung like the suit never reclaimed
from the dry cleaner's revolving track.
When did he turn skeletal? In the wind
sometimes, I'd hear un-nameable clatter.
Later, he hung like a flag of truce, mid-siege.
Or an amputee's knotted sleeve. Some days,
he hangs like drapes in a house fire—every saving
axe and hose, elsewhere employed. No.
My uncle hangs like the garfish
viewed by elbowing strangers, walking the city pier.
Next day, I am ambushed, gagging
over the stretched skin in a butcher's display.
Was it yesterday? I saw that man-shaped bolt
of lightning, singeing horizon. But it's today's
winter rain, the prayer flag's slump that recalls
a sloughed skin.

Nobody Says My Uncle's Name Anymore

Somebody locked that terrible box
before I could tuck two shells inside

Now   in my canopy bed like a boat
with its roof the color of breath
on a winter night
I can't see a single star to wish on
So I remember the misty end
of that day on the pier
when Dad knelt at the stern
to check the outboard motor
that starts with two yanks and a cough

Uncle Dunkel said *Thanks* and *Don't worry*
because he knew how to work it
That's when I saw the tattoo on his arm
with the name of his almost-wife
and how it moved when he pulled the cord
as if Verna was waving hello   *Hello*
not floating forever out of our lives

The moon rose behind the dam
and gloomster bats trailed us in swoops
like sparklers frizzling to smoke
before darkness swallows
the name you were writing
The wake made two hills of water
side by side   moving away from each other

They petered out
like they were never there at all

Words which are not

enough—despite our regrets
and longings—mound,
musty and swept together
like fallen leaves, crackling
with sorrow nearly

unspeakable. Where is solace
meant to settle cleanly as dew?
A life shatters, its hunger
for wholeness hopefully
drifting toward Mystery,

that pure, original spark
pulsing within
a vitality deeper than
we dare believe. Prayers may
falter, but know this:

though language flails
and has too often failed us,
even our questions
eventually intersect
the beguiling Love

that summoned this universe,
which, from our first
shuddering breath,
clear through forever, is already
here, calling our truest name.

Eldergirl, on One Knee, Finds a Snail

No matter how small the act,
A kindness is never wasted.

–Aesop

Cooling as dew, you ooze across my palm,
a luminous trail—as of a patient angel
tending the flayed. Don't bother. I don't want
your slow glue. Watch me mutely
thicken the walls of my shell, year after year.
You do. Hinged within your expanding house,
what does it cost to bequeath shimmer?
What is it like being sought for slime? I know
people gather your rich opalescence
to soothe the seething wound, minimize scars,
even regenerate aging skin. Why not
renew my brow, or sluice these boxy
grooves running nose to lips? In other words,
roll back time. If only you could.
And if this were a miracle
and your quicksilver ministration, true,
I would kneel beneath the sycamore tree
where they cut my uncle's body loose,
and I would smooth your essence 'round
and around his mangled throat, even now.

Roof, with No Weather Vane

I was young and now I am old . . .

How lovely is your dwelling place . . .

–Ps 37:25 NIV; Ps 84:1 NIV

Eldergirl Wakes, to Frost

All this festooning of eaves
and downspouts! Chimneys. Shingles.
Every edge. Who leaves behind
their breath, like a calling card
fished from the smock
of a wizened artist, with sable brushes
strapped to each hand, faceting
gutters and sycamore trees?
Who speed-rimes antennae
and trims the satellite dish
with crystalwork? Be it vapor or ice dam,
the unraveled lace of a snail,
all that was liquid, in the beginning,
resurfaces somewhere:
the rivers of Eden, the tears of Christ.

Maybe the dead leave us

a gift we cannot
  imagine, moving
    like water around reeds,

under an oil slick—
  a current that blurs
    memory's suspect alchemy

with all the goodbyes
  yet to be said, between
    their death, and ours.

Picture a portage through time,
  where we can un-shoulder
    our past and reemerge

carried. Maybe this is how
  we reclaim our lives: as if
    trust is the next vessel.

Along the Shore, Overnight

New toadstools
shoulder through
sodden grass
the way sorrows
emerge, one
after another. Pilgrim,
in a season doubly
scented by windfall
apples and creeping
rot, please sidestep
the lone wet leaf,
seed-pearled with dew,
like a fairy mirror
inside a dollhouse
with too many doors,
long abandoned.
Shifting glints
might call to mind
glimpses—unintended
harm from someone
who loved you
less well
than they meant to.
Let each pendulous
tremor, evoked
by your footfall,
nudge you toward
all that remains
unresolved,
unformed.

Eldergirl Ventures Another Look

Once, my whistling, blue-eyed uncle
arrived for tea like a daddy longlegs,
folding up, in our corner nook. I
prattled and poured orange pop
from a teapot the size of my fist. He
cradled his tiny turquoise cup
and never spilled.

Uncle Dunkel skipped rocks.
He jitterbugged. Shinnied up trees.
He was six-plus feet of living
lath held together by pluck
and sinew, a man who strode
along ridge poles, shingling
a roof like an urban card sharp
armed with a royal flush.
Cellar-to-roof, he could conjure
a whole house. On a break,
his Lucky Strike wizardry
wreathed my finger with smoke rings,
wobbly as vortices made by oars,
our two mouths frozen open.

My father said the barbed wire noose
stretched. And stretched.
Did Uncle Dunkel lunge
for an overhead bough? How long
can a soldier hold himself up,
above the ground? No. I will remember
him on the swing, kicking toward heaven,
those pale, narrow feet aloft.

Fowler House Redux

I
miss
small feet
sneaking out
a bedroom window,
onto our shingled roof,
hoarding, with you, the last of
the day's heat, hearing the dogleg
crank—sharing that song, our built-in
percussion. Listen with me: Home means
us, cellar-to-roof: aerial, eaves, downspout,
doorways, keyholes, even flights of stairs,
still standing, or not. Survivor, sprite, these
beams are shoulders for sorrows, held like
secret shadows and bones, in closets. I am
each source of heat. The light, that leaked,
your windowed wishing womb, in the hall.
A foundation, on loan, with landing strips
for fireflies. O travel back, in the name of
wingdom. Power, the continuing story . . .

Afterward

I will give you the treasures of darkness,
and the riches hidden in secret places . . .

–Isa 45:3 BSB

All that is Binding:
Eldergirl Finds the Book

It's ninety-seven years old. We creak
open the vintage cover. Cello tape
crackles and splits, the color
stark as my uncle's nicotine stains.
            My granddaughter, Chloe, turns
each brittle leaf like a treasure map.
I found it today, among Nana's linens—
the small Easter tale: between us now,
Mrs. Bunnykins' Busy Day unfolds . . .
            till a page drops out. "Why
is the little book broken?" Chloe asks.
"Somebody loved this story to pieces,"
I say. The small, water-colored world blurs
as I read the inscription, in Nana's hand.
            My breath is a thorn,
sounding out the words, with a child.
1934, For his fourth birthday:
This Book Belongs to
Donald Severson. A gift.

            For Donald (Uncle Dunkel) Severson, 1930–1964
            Corporal, United States Army

Notes

"Everything Begins in Water": this compelling line opened a sermon given by my pastor, Eric Peterson, author of *Wade in the Water* (Cascade Books, 2018).

"Seen from a Distance ...": Uncle Dunkel served in Korea from 1951–1953.

"What the Snapping Turtle Said": Paul J. Pastor's poem, "What the Spider Said" (*Bower Lodge*, Fernwood Press, 2021) inspired me to create the acrostic poems using the common or Latin name for each creature.

"What the Muskrat Said": *ha brakha dabra*, Hebrew for "the blessing has spoken," may be the origin of *abracadabra* (*The Book of Mysteries*, Jonathan Cahn, Frontline, 2016).

"Hindsight": Uncle Dunkel and my grandfather built the "scream" porch and remodeled the kitchen and many-doored shotgun hall. The ceiling light leaked the whole time I lived there.

"While Swimming Laps . . .": a shagbark hickory tree provided the leaves.

"Larkin's Mom, in Her Kitchen, at Twilight": *innocent as an egg* comes from *Delight*, J.B. Priestly's charming collection of essays (Great Northern, 60th Anniversary edition, 2009).

"Radiator": most rooms in Fowler House had one, sheathed in ornate metal housing. During the winter, I helped fill the trays with water.

"Dive . . .": the race is real; the river scene is emblematic of what some soldiers experienced in the Korean War. My father and uncle never talked to me about their wars. As a child, I acquired story fragments and impressions by eavesdropping.

"That Dark and Stormy Night . . .": Brahms was legendary in his vocal expression and range.

"Larkin and the Hope Chest": I still have it. The garfish appeared one summer only, a lead pipe of a fish my father eventually speared with a gaffe, then buried in Mom's rose garden.

"Belated Remembrance": I was inspired by Wendell Berry's famous poem, "The Peace of Wild Things" (*The Peace of Wild Things and Other Poems*, Penguin, 2018).

"Eldergirl, Running a Bath": Though secretive about finances, my enigmatic father loved the "teachable moment" and generously invested in my education, often by his own quiet example.

"The Psalm Formerly Known as *Swim* . . .": Korea is often called the forgotten war.

"Eldergirl, on the Mystery of Physics": words by physicist John Stamos launched this poem.

"Seen from a Distance . . .": Some sycamore trees die from the heart, outward.

"Eldergirl Imagines a Mourning . . .": *Selah* (found in Psalms and Habakkuk) may mean "to pause, to praise or lift up, to measure or weigh in the balances. Or it may indicate a musical direction." The initial phrases of my avian invitation echo the number of notes and stresses in the mourning dove's signature song.

"Profile": as a child I was taught suicide was unforgiveable. I no longer believe this.

"*Dunkelheit*": this poem was inspired by Yusef Kumunyakaa's poem, "You and I Are Disappearing—Björn Håkansson" (*Dien Cai Dau*, Wesleyan University Press, 1988). Strange as it seems, finding apt comparisons proved therapeutic; it helped defuse long-buried horror.

Acknowledgments

For the nails, then and now,
for each day's hinges, dusk through dawn,
and for the easing oil:
all praise to God,
who repairs and restores the soul,
and who meets us at each reopened door.

To Fowler House, with your bold turquoise door: you enfolded me; you hold me, still.

To the gifted, beautiful, wounded humans who gave me life and loved me, from my first breath, to their last: dear Mom and Dad, rest in peace.

To my dynamo sister, Carol, who helped me count the doors and sort through the baggage: I can't imagine this world without you.

To Randy, beloved brother in heaven, who nicknamed our favorite uncle: I miss you.

To Uncle Dunkel, my first hero: I wish everyone, everywhere could know you.

To Will, our children and grandchildren: my heart and hands, always.

To Mark Doty: your visionary teaching and generous input undergird this endeavor.

To D.S. Martin: Thank you for your masterful attention to meaning's rigor and beauty. You set a deep healing in motion.

To Susan Cowger: I cherish your matchless companionship in faith and in artistry. Thank you for caring for me and my family as well as my writing. Here's to the next endeavor . . .

Endless thanks to generous and gifted friends, reviewers, interviewers, editors, endorsers, and fellow wordsmiths who continually help me grow: Eric and Elizabeth Peterson, core group, Wednesday Writers, Kingdom Poets, my loyal blog community, CPC Book Group, L.L. Barkat, and the intrepid zoom sisterhood of the golden shawl.

To my readers: I treasure the gift of your thoughtful attention.

To the dedicated Wipf & Stock team at Cascade Books, especially George Callihan, Shannon Carter, Ian Creeger, EJ Davila, and Sierra Jackson: my profound thanks for your expertise, generous patience, and creative vision.

Lastly, I am grateful to the editors of the following publications, in which these poems first appeared, sometimes in different form. Thank you for believing in my work.

Beautiful Things at *River Teeth Journal:* "Dam"

Books & Culture: "Eldergirl Remembers the Magi," formerly titled "Epiphany"

Eastern Iowa Review: "Almost a Way to Say Sorry," formerly titled "Scapegoat"

Ekstasis: "Seen from a Distance: Father, Daughter, Uncle"

Every Day Poems: "Peripheral" and "The Secret Bellyfoot Opera, under the Dining Room Windows," formerly titled "A Walk, a Rout, an Escargatoire"

Foreshadow: "There must be a way to listen"; "A House like a Shawl," formerly titled "Uphill"; and "What the Snail Said"

Heliotrope: "Orison, in One's Seventh Decade," formerly titled "Lakeside"

Mid-American Review: "Eldergirl Tries to Imagine Verna, Uncle Dunkel's Fiancée, in Her Kitchen," formerly titled "Rainworms"

Natural Bridge: "Eldergirl Ventures Another Look," formerly titled "A Silence I Keep Falling Through"

Pure in Heart: "The Psalm Formerly Known as *Swim*, for Two Voices (then and now)," formerly titled "Kid Larkin and the Psalm Formerly Known as *Swim*"

Reformed Journal: "Along the Shore, Overnight," formerly titled "You Could Call This Mercy"

Relief: "Belated Remembrance," formerly titled "Lately, When I Awake Desolate"

Ruminate: "Eldergirl, Running a Bath," formerly titled "Children Will Swim Here"

Rust & Moth: "Hindsight" and "While Swimming Laps, Eldergirl Remembers Her Tree House"

San Pedro River Review: "Larkin, in Bed with the Flu, Relives that Day at the River, without Her Dog"

The Christian Century: "What the Muskrat Said"

The Christian Courier: "Eldergirl Wakes, to Frost," formerly titled "Frost"

The Clayjar Review: "Everything Begins in Water" and "Larkin's Mom, Kneeling, in Her Bedroom," formerly titled "Rookie Mom, Kneeling, in Her Bedroom"

The Curator: "Between Tables"; "Larkin's Mom, in the Kitchen, at Twilight"; and the forthcoming "Fowler House Redux," to be titled "House"

The Spokane Review: "Eldergirl, on Forgetting," formerly titled "A Tree Shadowed the Room Where He told Her"

Wordfest Anthology: "About Barbs, Then and Now," formerly titled "War Pies"

"Orison, in One's Seventh Decade" also appeared in *Bodies of Water, Bodies of Flesh*

"Eldergirl Remembers the Magi" also appeared in *Adam, Eve, and the Riders of the Apocalypse*; *The Catholic Poetry Room*; and *Abbey of the Arts, Featured Poet*

"A House Like a Shawl" also appeared in *Poems for Ephesians*

"About Barbs, Then and Now" is forthcoming in *Rooted: Arboreal Nonfiction*.

Permissions

The Poiema Poetry Series

COLLECTIONS IN THIS SERIES INCLUDE:

Six Sundays Toward a Seventh by Sydney Lea
Epitaphs for the Journey by Paul Mariani
Within This Tree of Bones by Robert Siegel
Particular Scandals by Julie L. Moore
Gold by Barbara Crooker
A Word In My Mouth by Robert Cording
Say This Prayer into the Past by Paul Willis
Scape by Luci Shaw
Conspiracy of Light by D.S. Martin
Second Sky by Tania Runyan
Remembering Jesus by John Leax
What Cannot Be Fixed by Jill Pelaez Baumgaertner
Still Working It Out by Brad Davis
The Hatching of the Heart by Margo Swiss
Collage of Seoul by Jae Newman
Twisted Shapes of Light by William Jolliff
These Intricacies by David Harrity
Where the Sky Opens by Laurie Klein
True, False, None of the Above by Marjorie Maddox
The Turning Aside anthology edited by D.S. Martin
Falter by Marjorie Stelmach
Phases by Mischa Willett
Second Bloom by Anya Krugovoy Silver
Adam, Eve, & the Riders of the Apocalypse anthology edited by D.S. Martin
Your Twenty-First Century Prayer Life by Nathaniel Lee Hansen
Habitation of Wonder by Abigail Carroll
Ampersand by D.S. Martin
Full Worm Moon by Julie L. Moore
Ash & Embers by James A. Zoller
The Book of Kells by Barbara Crooker
Reaching Forever by Philip C. Kolin
The Book of Bearings by Diane Glancy
In a Strange Land anthology edited by D.S. Martin

What I Have I Offer With Two Hands by Jacob Stratman
Slender Warble by Susan Cowger
Madonna, Complex by Jen Stewart Fueston
No Reason by Jack Stewart
Abundance by Andrew Lansdown
Angelicus by D.S. Martin
Trespassing on the Mount of Olives by Brad Davis
The Angel of Absolute Zero by Marjorie Stelmach
Duress by Karen An-hwei Lee
Wolf Intervals by Graham Hillard
To Heaven's Rim anthology edited by Burl Horniachek
Cup My Days Like Water by Abigail Carroll
Soon Done with the Crosses by Claude Wilkinson
Hawk & Songbird by Susan Cowger

All author profits from the sale of this book will be donated to Habit for Humanity.

Learn more, sign up to volunteer your time (no experience necessary), or make a secure donation toward safe, well-designed, affordable shelter for others at https://www.habitat.org/

Thank you for reading this book! I hope you'll visit my monthly blog at www.lauriekleinscribe.com

www.ingramcontent.com/pod-product-compliance
Lightning Source LLC
LaVergne TN
LVHW041301080426
835510LV00009B/831